JARROW
HISTORY TOUR

To the people of Jarrow for their continued encouragement and support.

First published 2019

Amberley Publishing
The Hill, Stroud,
Gloucestershire, GL5 4EP
www.amberley-books.com

Copyright © Paul Perry, 2019
Map contains Ordnance Survey data
© Crown copyright and database
right [2019]

The right of Paul Perry to be
identified as the Author of this work
has been asserted in accordance with
the Copyrights, Designs and Patents
Act 1988.

ISBN 978 1 4456 5211 5 (print)
ISBN 978 1 4456 5212 2 (ebook)

British Library Cataloguing in
Publication Data.
A catalogue record for this book is
available from the British Library.

Origination by Amberley Publishing.
Printed in Great Britain.

INTRODUCTION

Since the invention of the tiny camera most of us now have them built into our mobile phones. We have turned into a nation of photographers, taking pictures of anything that tickles our fancy, especially taking endless images of our loved ones and capturing cherished moments. We treasure photographs of people we love and save them with pictures of ourselves for posterity. Practically everyone has had his or her photograph taken at one time or another. Walking down the street, driving our cars, in supermarkets, most of these cameras are visible, although others are not so, but many have one thing in common: they are generally present for our safety.

The old adage 'the camera never lies' is now way out of date. This may have been true several years ago when film cameras were used, and prints were produced in a darkened room. However, with the development of the digital camera and photo manipulation software, the adage should now read 'the camera lies quite often'. Changing technologies transform the way photography is perceived. Today's revolution is nothing more than the latest episode in its evolution.

The whole conception of photography is due to early pioneers such as Fox Talbot, Niépce and, of course, Daguerre during the 1800s. Prior to the development of the hand-held camera and faster film, it was difficult for these photographers to freeze time.

Street photographers, as they were called, concentrated their efforts photographing buildings and the urban landscape, creating images to record the way they saw the world around them on cumbersome tripod-mounted plate cameras, producing sepia-toned images that had become a particular, and familiar, form of representation. Great photographs are endlessly interesting because the factual content they contain is timeless, variations of which produce a fascinating and diverse range of unforgettable images.

This document – an abridged and updated version of an earlier publication from 2008, *Jarrow Through Time* – is the outcome of a careful selection of additional images of Jarrow in a geographical format. I have chosen familiar and classic images from my collection, together with photographs that are unknown or rarely seen. Thanks to the pains of those early street photographers, we have a true untainted, unmanipulated perspective of the past. Modern-day technology means we never quite know what is a true image and what has been tampered with. Will the authenticity of these photographs qualify as a reliable record of how things truly were? Will future generations be able to rely on images taken over the last few decades as a true representation of life at the time? Probably not!

KEY

1. Monkton Village
2. The Grange, Monkton Village
3. Butchers Bridge Road
4. York Avenue
5. Bede Burn Road
6. Croft Terrace
7. Park Road
8. West Park
9. North View
10. Hill Street
11. Grant Street
12. Station Stairs
13. Palmer Street
14. Western Road
15. Ellison Street
16. Station Street
17. Palmer Memorial Statue
18. Ormonde Street
19. Ferry Street
20. St Peter's Church
21. Pedestrian Tunnel
22. Pearson Place
23. Commercial Road
24. North Street
25. Walter Street
26. Grange Road West
27. Clayton Street
28. Christ Church
29. St John's Terrace
30. Monkton Road
31. Chapel Road
32. Cambrian Street
33. Grange Road
34. Staple Road
35. High Street
36. Curlew Road
37. Quay Corner
38. Cuthbert Terrace
39. Jarrow Hall
40. Drewett Playing Fields
41. St Paul's Church Rectory
42. St Paul's Church
43. Bede's Chair
44. Monastery Ruins
45. Tyne Tunnel
46. Dee Street
47. Monkton Terrace
48. Monkton Road
49. Howard Street
50. Henry Street

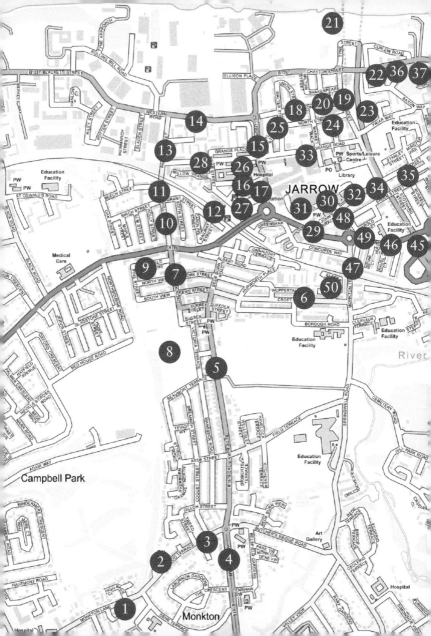

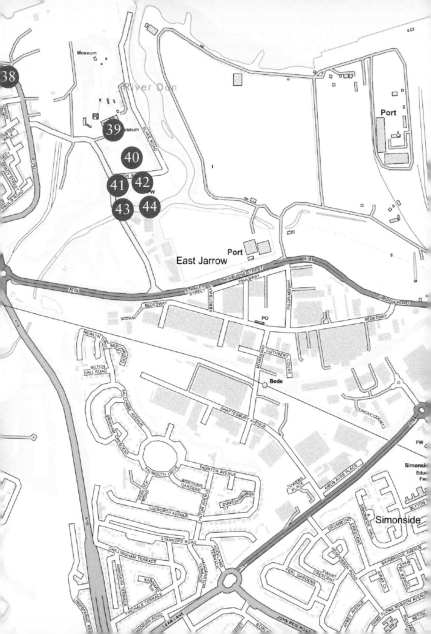

Monkton.

1. MONKTON VILLAGE

The sleepy and ancient little village of Monkton, nestled between Jarrow and Hebburn, has for many centuries been associated with the Venerable Bede, and reputed to be his place of birth. In more modern times, the Lord Nelson Inn, in the centre of this photograph from 1906, dates from 1870. However, the original building was demolished around 1934 and replaced with the building we are more familiar with today.

2. THE GRANGE, MONKTON VILLAGE

The Grange, dating from 1539 and situated in Monkton Village, was constructed as a single-storey residence. In 1662, its owner Richard Marshall made considerable changes to the building, increasing the value of the property and more than doubling its value to £150. This substantial increase in value was due to the addition of a second storey. The residence as it stands today was completed around 1773, and is justifiably the oldest residence in Jarrow.

3. BUTCHERS BRIDGE ROAD

Many explanations as to the origin of the name of this thoroughfare have surfaced over the years, but all have been discarded as inconclusive. More than 150 years ago, this part of Jarrow was largely taken over by farmland and cornfields covered the area extensively. This image from 1955 was taken from Wood Terrace, showing the junction with York Avenue and Butchers Bridge Road to the left. The perimeter wall (pictured) was built around wasteland during the 1930s, which prevented the council making claim to it. In 1958, the land was used for the construction of St Matthew's Church.

4. YORK AVENUE

Prior to the construction of York Avenue, and in keeping with the surrounding area, this site was predominantly used for agricultural purposes. The construction of social housing commenced around 1920, concluding at its junction with Valley View. Beyond this point the land was given over for the development of private housing. During the 1990s this elegant and picturesque dual carriageway – opened in 1928 by HRH Duchess of York – was partially reduced to single carriageway status, thus creating residential parking.

5. BEDE BURN ROAD

During the 1950s and '60s, Jarrow was subject to substantial refurbishment, both in the town centre and the outskirts. Very welcome post-war housing was being constructed as promised by the government. Around the same time, many places of worship were greatly in need of repair but insufficient revenue and lack of public subscription prevented this. As a consequence, many churches were demolished. However, some did survive the marauding bands of demolition men. One in particular, Park Methodist Church (pictured to the left of this Victorian image), did but sadly was devastated by fire during the latter part of 2017.

6. CROFT TERRACE

The desirable Victorian terrace to the left of this 1950s photograph looks almost the same as it did when first built towards the end of the nineteenth century. However, the houses to the right of this elegant thoroughfare were partially demolished during the 1960s in favour of a more up to date municipal housing complex. The absence of vehicular traffic in this charming image illustrates precisely how our thoroughfares have changed in the last fifty years or so.

7. PARK ROAD

The imposing Victorian houses in Park Road look as good today as they did when first built towards the end of the nineteenth century. The foundation stone of the Church of the Good Shepherd, to the right of this image from 1906, was laid by Mrs Bee, wife of the vicar of Christ Church in 1886. The 300-seat building was financed and gifted to the town by Lord and Lady Northbourne. The church, which was demolished during the 1970s, was built to meet the needs of the rising population and reduce the pressure on Christ Church. Apart from the ever-increasing volumes of traffic, little has changed in this part of town.

8. WEST PARK

West Park, more commonly known as 'Ducks Park', was gifted to the town by Sir Walter and Lady James, latterly Lord and Lady Northbourne, in 1876. One year later, a drinking fountain was erected at the entrance in 1877, a gift from confectioner and Councillor Alderman Thomas Sheldon. Volunteers tend it to a very high standard; the beautiful and colourful floral displays all summer long make the parkland a very pleasant place to be.

9. NORTH VIEW

Another interesting little picture from a bygone era. This time North View, where time and change seem to have passed us by. This lovely terrace of fine residences remains exactly as it did when Victoria ruled.

10. HILL STREET

The railway bridge in the centre of this 1950s photograph of Hill Street was constructed in 1872, the same year as the LNER passenger and mineral line rail link to South Shields opened. Today the route from Newcastle to South Shields is serviced by a rapid-transit system Tyne & Wear Metro, operated by Nexus. The buildings to the left were occupied by Jarrow and Hebburn Co-operative Society bakery and dairy divisions.

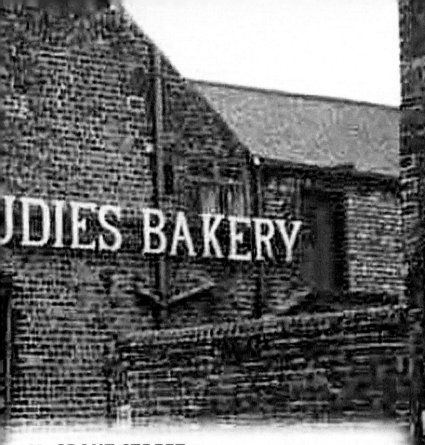

11. GRANT STREET

While the majority of Grant Street was residential with terraced accommodation, there was a tiny assortment of shops catering for residents' requirements. Gaudies Bakery (pictured), McPherson's hairdressers and Frank Walkes newsagents survived here until the majority of the area was demolished during the 1960s. This area is now occupied by a social club.

12. STATION STAIRS

When this crossing over the railway lines was constructed in 1872, it was by no means the structure portrayed in this image from 1960. Originally, it was a simple elevated walkway without the canopy. Some years later elaborate plans to enhance the structure were submitted by LNER but were abandoned when planning permission was refused. The council did, however, permit the walkway to be fitted with glass-sided panels supporting a tiled roof. The structure was demolished during the 1970s in favour of a more substantial crossing, what we know today as the Metro bridge.

13. PALMER STREET

Gaslights, cobblestones and paving slabs, the absence of double-yellow lines and road markings in Palmer Street was typical of Jarrow Streets during the 1950s. These rows of dimly lit terraced houses were built by Palmer for his workforce and situated conveniently close to his shipbuilding empire. The houses were demolished by the 1960s, and the land was eventually given over for use as a business park.

14. WESTERN ROAD

The area surrounding Western Road has a very long history of industrial activity. This image from 1970 shows the former site of the Jarrow Metals Industry, a company created by John Jarvis in 1938 specialising in the manufacture of components for the shipbuilding industry. The Davy Roll Company purchased the foundry in 1968 and continued in the tradition of general engineering until the 1980s, when the land was reclaimed for further development.

15. ELLISON STREET

This image was taken at the junction of Ellison Street and Ormonde Street in 1952. The character of the thoroughfare remains much the same as it did when it was built towards the end of the nineteenth century, similar to that of the town centre. Ormonde Street to the left was totally transformed from the main shopping area to an assortment of modern homes in the 1960s, after the inauguration of the Arndale Centre.

16. STATION STREET

Formerly heavily populated with terraced accommodation, Station Street, pictured here in 1988, and nearby Sheldon Street were devastated by enemy bombing during the Second World War, culminating in a substantial loss of life. This eventually saw the demolition of several houses in the area. A plaque of remembrance commemorating the atrocity was erected close by. Northern General Transport constructed a bus depot and garage on the former site in 1953.

17. PALMER MEMORIAL STATUE

This bronze statue of Sir Charles was erected within the grounds of the hospital he created for his workforce in recognition of his achievement as a shipbuilding magnate in 1904. During the late 1970s, the statue was relocated to a site overlooking his beloved River Tyne. In 2007, after several bouts of vandalism, it was refurbished and repositioned at a site in Grange Road overlooking the town hall, a position befitting a great industrialist who was elected as the first mayor of the town in 1875.

18. ORMONDE STREET

This lovely photograph of Ormonde Street from 1955 typifies precisely how the shops possessed their own individual fascia, charm and character. Today these tumbledown buildings nevertheless seem so much more appealing than the precincts and shopping malls of today. Sadly, these charming shops are no more than distant memories on a few tattered old photographs, but with their help the memories of them will last forever.

19. FERRY STREET

Ferry Street as photographed by James Hunter Carr in 1954. The derelict land pictured was known as Weavers Row centuries earlier, as the surrounding area was industrialised with sailmakers during the time of sailing ships. Eventually, as sail made way for steam, the area became prolific as a pottery. The flats to the right of the image were the final buildings to disappear from Drury Lane. The building to the extreme right was St Peter's church hall, which was also demolished around the same time.

20. ST PETER'S CHURCH

Built in Chaytor Street in 1881, the 400-seat St Peter's Church, complete with a spire measuring 120 feet, originally covered an area of 500 square yards. The spire was extensively damaged during the Second World War when a wandering airship broke free from its moorings in a nearby gas yard, colliding with the church. Finances prohibited the restoration of the damaged building, but levelling the spire became an acceptable and affordable alternative.

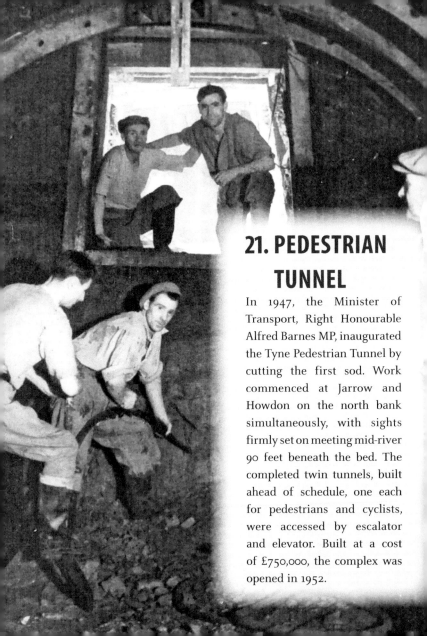

21. PEDESTRIAN TUNNEL

In 1947, the Minister of Transport, Right Honourable Alfred Barnes MP, inaugurated the Tyne Pedestrian Tunnel by cutting the first sod. Work commenced at Jarrow and Howdon on the north bank simultaneously, with sights firmly set on meeting mid-river 90 feet beneath the bed. The completed twin tunnels, built ahead of schedule, one each for pedestrians and cyclists, were accessed by escalator and elevator. Built at a cost of £750,000, the complex was opened in 1952.

22. PEARSON PLACE

This photograph from 1950 was taken in Pearson Place, showing an area known as the pit heap. The 'pit heap' was created with earth removed from an area during the construction of the Alfred Pit, which dates from the beginning of the nineteenth century. To the right of the image we see another image of St Peter's church hall and in the centre is the Golden Fleece public house, one of two sharing the same name. The other was in Ferry Street.

23. COMMERCIAL ROAD

This fascinating photograph from 1904 shows another aspect of track laying for the forthcoming tram service, which commenced two years later in 1906 and operated smoothly and efficiently ferrying men back and forth to work for many years. The image was taken in Staple Road at the junction of Grange Road and Buddle Street, and clearly shows the track's progress along Commercial Road.

24. NORTH STREET

In 1882, the Jarrow and Hebburn Co-operative Society opened a department store and tearooms in North Street. However, the department store was devastated by fire in 1906. After restoration and partial reconstruction of the building it was once again ready for business by 1910. Pictured in this very busy image from 1950 are the Picture House (extreme left), post office and Jarrow & Hebburn Co-op department store.

25. WALTER STREET

The public swimming baths in Walter Street opened in 1911 for the purpose of recreation and swimming instruction. Bathing facilities were provided for townsfolk living in accommodation without adequate sanitation. The building, pictured in 1966, was demolished during the 1970s as more modern facilities became available at South Shields and Hebburn.

26. GRANGE ROAD WEST

Although the premises of the Shields Gas Company has changed hands many times over the years, the fascia remains much the same as it did when this photograph was taken in 1912. The buildings to the right of the image were demolished during the 1950s in preparation for shopping precincts.

27. CLAYTON STREET

The Palmer Memorial Hospital in this image from 1906 was built in 1870 as a memorial to Palmer's first wife, Jane, who did so much for the welfare of the people of Jarrow. A commemorative stained-glass window, depicting biblical scenes of charitable acts involving women, was on display at the hospital's main entrance, and is now incorporated within the new hospital as a lasting memory. The war memorial, also situated in Clayton Street, was gifted to the town by the Palmer's in 1921.

28. CHRIST CHURCH

In 1863, prior to the creation of the parish and construction of Christ Church, services were conducted in local schoolrooms and in 1868 Revd John Bee was appointed rector of the recently formed Jarrow Grange parish. In 1869 and with financial backing again courtesy of Sir Walter and Lady Sarah James, the church was constructed, consecrated and made ready for worshipers soon after. The tower and spire, complete with six bells, were added to the structure in 1882. To celebrate the golden jubilee of the church in 1919, two additional bells were added, making a full peal of eight.

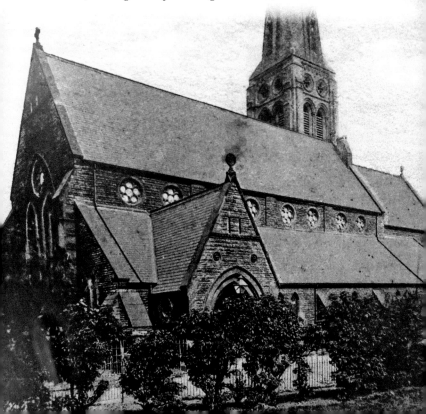

29. ST JOHN'S TERRACE

It is difficult to imagine that this tranquil image of St John's Terrace was a major bus route both in and out of town when this photograph was taken in 1955. Buses were introduced to Jarrow at the demise of the electric tram system in 1929, having served the town for no less than twenty-three years. From this time public transport was in the hands of Charlton & Co., who operated a successful and efficient transport system until Northern General Transport took over in 1932. The elegant terrace has changed considerably in recent years, but some of the fine old properties to the left survive today.

30. MONKTON ROAD

Another lovely image of disappearing Jarrow, this time Monkton Road, around 1955. After its demolition the land lay barren for several years until building commenced with the construction of the Salvation Army Citadel, the post office, which relocated from premises in North Street, and the Branch Library. In the meantime, the land in the foreground was being prepared for the Arndale Centre. In 2019, the public library relocated once again, this time to Jarrow Focus, a fitness and entertainment facility in the town centre.

31. CHAPEL ROAD

Another central area, covering a 10-acre site, earmarked for clearance to make way for the Arndale Centre was the tiny cottages in Caledonian Road, Charles Street and Hibernian Road, which are visible in this 1955 image from Chapel Road. The decision was taken to destroy row upon row of the cottages in a controlled blaze. This task was undertaken by Durham County Fire Brigade in 1955. Today, after further development, the site is occupied by a supermarket.

32. CAMBRIAN STREET

A classic example of the old and the new coming together in this image of Cambrian Street from 1953. The Festival Flats, a complex of eighty-four apartments constructed as Jarrow's contribution to commemorate the Festival of Britain in 1951, are clearly visible to the right of the image. This complex of modern housing heralded a new beginning of modern self-contained accommodation for Jarrow. To the left are the ageing properties of Gray Street and Burns Street, which were demolished around 1958. The building in the centre was Dunn Street School, which was severely damaged during an air attack in 1941.

33. GRANGE ROAD

Another classic image from 1954, depicting the town as it was and fondly remembered by many. This time it is of Grange Road looking toward the town hall to the right and Christ Church in the centre. Built in 1902 and 1869 respectively, these are the only two buildings in the photograph still survive today. Formerly called the Kino, the Regal cinema was a former washhouse and furniture warehouse that was converted into a theatre in 1908.

34. STAPLE ROAD

Having set themselves in the forefront of education by being first in the field with new schools under the Education Act of 1870, the Jarrow School Board were to add to the successful opening of two schools by adding a third. A site was purchased from wealthy landowner Ormonde Drewett. Initially the new school was to be called 'The Eastern School' but governing bodies voted against it in favour of 'Dunn Street Government School', which opened in 1874. This photograph showing the schoolhouse and entrance to the school to the left was taken from Staple Road in 1954.

35. HIGH STREET

Demolished during the 1930s, these white-walled miners' cottages were constructed by industrialist Simon Temple in 1804 to accommodate his small army of miners who toiled relentlessly at the coalface, in deplorable conditions, surfacing the precious black fuel, the majority of which was transported to London. Notorious Australian outlaw Ned Kelly's parents were reputed to have resided here for some time after leaving Ireland en route to Australia.

36. CURLEW ROAD

This 1950s image of Curlew Road was taken from the old gasometer. This area was severely damaged during a bombing raid in 1941 during the Second World War. This devastating blow to the town resulted in the demolition of several houses. These were replaced with modern-style houses during the 1950s. In the background are the remains of the cottages in Stead Street and High Street. The penned area in the bottom right of the image was the Jarrow branch of the Sea Cadet Corps, who are still active in the area today.

37. QUAY CORNER

A steady growth in river traffic passing this way on the lucrative waters of the River Tyne prompted the inauguration of a shipyard specialising in the repair of merchant and naval vessels. The Mercantile Dry Dock and Engineering Co. was created in 1885. The buildings in this image from the 1930s were eventually demolished in favour of a smart new office block for an oil storage terminal.

TO THE MERCANTILE
DRY DOCK Co LTD

38. CUTHBERT TERRACE

Cuthbert Terrace, also referred to as Church Bank, was situated close to Jarrow Hall. Home to pit owner Simon Temple, it is just visible to the right of this image from 1945. This former residence lay derelict for several years until the council utilised it for storage during the 1970s. Soon after the row of terraced houses (left) were demolished, the area was reclaimed and converted into a replica of an Anglo-Saxon farm and museum, Bede's World Heritage Centre.

39. JARROW HALL

After lying uninhabited and almost derelict for several years, Jarrow Hall was the former residence of industrialist Simon Temple. In a desperate bid to prevent the building, which dates from 1785, from being demolished, the council stepped in and utilised the decaying building for storage from 1935 until 1974. From this time the building was converted into the Bede Monastery Museum. Today the museum is known as Jarrow Hall Anglo-Saxon Farm and Heritage Centre, and, as the name suggests, the popular venue demonstrates Anglo-Saxon life in this part of Britain.

40. DREWETT PLAYING FIELDS

The Drewett Playing Fields in the east end of the town were opened in 1912. The site was gifted to the town by landowner Alfred Henry Chaytor, who inherited the Jarrow Hall estate from his late uncle Drewett Ormonde Drewett, after whom the recreation facility is named. Soon after the opening ceremony, Charles Harrison was appointed to maintain the standards of the parkland laid down by Chaytor. From this time the park has always been known as 'Charlie's Park'.

41. ST PAUL'S CHURCH RECTORY

This quite old photograph of St Paul's Rectory, situated close to the church, was taken soon after its completion. The rare image is likely to be one of a kind. While the church dates from the seventh century, the rectory was built in 1855. However, it was demolished in 1878 after a lifespan of only twenty-three years. No records survive as to why the building was demolished. From around the time of the demolition the rectory was relocated to Borough Road in the town centre.

42. ST PAUL'S CHURCH

The chancel of St Paul's Church was founded in AD 681 prior to the arrival of Bede. The basilica was built later in the decade, and for many years they were two separate structures until the construction of the tower in 685, the same year the church was dedicated to St Paul. It was from this time the basilica and chancel were recognised as one building.

43. BEDE'S CHAIR

Within the parish church of St Paul, sitting rather awkwardly, is a crudely built little wooden chair that is thought to have belonged to Bede. For centuries it was believed the chair possessed mystical powers and anyone sitting in it would be miraculously cured of any illness they may have. There was also a strong belief the chair held a cure for infertility. These legends have been passed down from generation to generation, although Bede's bottom never actually graced the ancient relic; carbon dating revealed the oak wood chair was made during the eleventh century.

44. MONASTERY RUINS

It was to the cloisters of this seventh-century monastery that Bede was taken to aged just seven years, where he lived worshipped and worked until his death in AD 735, probably from asthma, aged sixty-two. This multilingual genius had mastered every aspect of every subject known to man at that time. This image from an engraving of the abandoned monastery dates from the twelfth century, stands as a testament to our heritage, and holds the privilege of being one of the oldest buildings in the country.

45. TYNE TUNNEL

Plans for a vehicular tunnel beneath the River Tyne had been in place since 1955. In the interim period that followed, and after contracts were signed, work eventually commenced in 1960. Despite several setbacks the tunnel was completed ahead of schedule and officially opened by HRH Queen Elizabeth in October 1967. Excavations for a sister tunnel commenced in 2008. The Queen returned to the area in 2012 to perform the official opening. Pictured is the entrance to the original tunnel under construction in 1960.

46. DEE STREET

The former Dee Street was situated precisely where the Jarrow entrance to the Tyne Tunnel was to be sited. Consequently, a substantial part of the accommodation in the immediate vicinity was demolished. This image of the property in Dee Street dates from 1949.

47. MONKTON TERRACE

During the 1960s, Jarrow was undergoing major refurbishment. Row upon row of substandard accommodation was being torn down. The terraced houses in Monkton Terrace, pictured here in 1945, were vacated and eventually demolished around the middle of the 1960s, making way for yet another housing complex. The Epinay estate was named after Jarrow's twin town Épinay-sur-Seine.

48. MONKTON ROAD

Opened in 1868 in Monkton Road, St Bede's School was primarily for the education of infant children. By the end of the 1960s and greatly in need of repair, the building was demolished and replaced with modern facilities in Staple Road. Eventually around 2006 this building was also demolished as the land it occupied was required for the Tyne Tunnel project.

49. HOWARD STREET

Constructed on a triangular site at Harold Street and Howard Street, St Bede's RC School dates from 1912, when the dedication stone was placed in position. Built on the site of a former clay pit, the £10,000 building with places for 1,000 children was officially opened in 1914. The school was divided into two departments: the upper floors were initially used for junior boys and girls, and the ground floors for seniors. This arrangement created two separate schools within a single building. The boys gained access to the school via Harold Street and the girls at Howard Street.

50. HENRY STREET

The former Henry Street was situated straddling Monkton Terrace and Albert Road. The tiny cottages hugged either side of this well-cared-for thoroughfare, where women polished the front doorstep with 'rubby stone', a chalk-like substance. It has been decades since the cottages were demolished but are fondly remembered by those who inhabited them. This photograph dates from 1945.

ACKNOWLEDGMENTS

I would like to extend my gratitude to the following individuals and organisations who assisted in the preparation of this document: Angela and Oliver Snowden, Anthony and Malcolm Perry, Kevin Donnelly, Lisa Nightingale, David Morton, Revd Gerard Martin, Lawrence Cuthbert, Lorrain and Andrew Hillas, the *Shields Gazette*, NCJ Media, Amberley Publishing and South Tyneside Libraries.